Chants

Primary Concepts®

Editor: Nancy Tune
Illustrations: John Palacios
Design and Production: Candace Wesen

©2005 Primary Concepts

Cat. No. 3834
ISBN: 1-893791-35-1

Contents

One, Two, Buckle My Shoe

1   One, two,

2   Buckle my shoe.

3   Three, four,

4   Shut the door.

1   Five, six,

2   Pick up sticks.

3   Seven, eight,

4   Lay them straight.

1   Nine, ten,

2   A big fat hen.

Teddy Bear, Teddy Bear

All   Teddy bear, teddy bear,

1   Turn around.

All   Teddy bear, teddy bear,

2   Touch the ground.

All   Teddy bear, teddy bear,

3   Touch your shoe.

All   Teddy bear, teddy bear,

All   THAT WILL DO.

All   Teddy bear, teddy bear,

1   Go upstairs.

All   Teddy bear, teddy bear,

2   Say your prayers.

All   Teddy bear, teddy bear,

3   Turn out the light.

All   Teddy bear, teddy bear,

All   Say good night.

The Song of Popcorn

All   Pop, pop, pop!

1   Says the popcorn in the pan.

All   Pop, pop, pop!

2   You can catch me if you can.

All   Pop, pop, pop!

3   Says each kernel hard and yellow.

All   Pop, pop, pop!

4   I'm a dancing little fellow.

All   Pop, pop, pop!

1   How I scamper through the heat.

All   Pop, pop, pop!

2   You will find me good to eat.

All   Pop, pop, pop!

3   I can whirl and skip and hop.

4   Pop! Pop! Pop! Pop!

All   POP! POP! POP!

One, Two, Three, Four, Five

All	One, two, three, four, five,
1	Once I caught a fish alive.
All	Six, seven, eight, nine, ten,
2	Then I let it go again.
All	Why did you let it go?
2	Because it bit my finger so.
1	Which finger did it bite?
2	The little finger on the right.

Alphabet Talk 1

1   A, B, C, D,

2   E, F, G,

3   H, I , J, K,

4   L, M, N, O, P,

1   Q, R, S,

2   T, U, V,

3   W, X,

4   Y and Z.

Alphabet Talk 2

1   A, B, C, D?

2   E, F, G!

3   H, I , J, K?

4   L, M, N, O, P.

1   Q, R, S?

2   T, U, V?

3   W, X,

4   Y and Z!

Alphabet Talk 3

1   A, B.

2   C, D.

3   E, F, G?

4   H, I, J, K.

1   L, M,

2   N, O, P.

3   Q, R, S!

4   T, U, V!

All   W, X?

All   Y and Z!

Miss Mary Mack

1	Miss Mary Mack, <u>Mack, Mack,</u>	<u>All</u>
2	All dressed in black, <u>black, black</u>	<u>All</u>
3	With silver buttons, <u>buttons, buttons</u>	<u>All</u>
4	Down her back, <u>back, back.</u>	<u>All</u>

1	She asked her mother, <u>mother, mother</u>	<u>All</u>
2	For fifty cents, <u>cents, cents</u>	<u>All</u>
3	To see the elephants, <u>elephants, elephants</u>	<u>All</u>
4	Jump the fence, <u>fence, fence.</u>	<u>All</u>

1 They jumped so high, <u>high, high,</u> <u>All</u>

2 They reached the sky, <u>sky, sky,</u> <u>All</u>

3 And never came back, <u>back, back</u> <u>All</u>

4 Till the fourth of July, <u>-ly, -ly.</u> <u>All</u>

The Dark House

1   In a dark, dark wood,

2   There was a dark, dark house,

1   And in that dark, dark house,

2   There was a dark, dark room,

1   And in that dark, dark room,

2   There was a dark, dark cupboard,

1   And in that dark, dark cupboard,

2   There was a dark, dark shelf,

1   And in that dark, dark shelf,

2   There was a dark, dark box,

1   And in that dark, dark box,

All   There was a GHOST!

Miss Polly Had a Dolly

1   Miss Polly had a dolly

     Who was sick, sick, sick,

2   So she called for the doctor

     To come quick, quick, quick.

3   The doctor came

     With his bag and his hat,

4   And he knocked at the door

     With a rat-a-tat-tat.

1   He looked at the dolly

    And he shook his head,

2   And he said, "Miss Polly,

    Put her straight to bed."

3   He wrote on a paper

    For a pill, pill, pill.

4   "That'll make her better,

    Yes it will, will, will!"

Fire! Fire!

1   "Fire! Fire!"

2   Cried Mrs. McGuire.

3   "Where? Where?"

4   Cried Mrs. Blair.

1   "All over town!"

2   Cried Mrs. Brown.

3   "Get some water!"

4   Cried her daughter.

1   "We'd better jump!"

2   Cried Mrs. Gump.

3   "It looks too risky!"

4   Cried Mrs. Matriski.

1   "What'll we do?"

2   Cried Mrs. LaRue.

3   "Turn in the alarm,"

4   Said Mrs. Parm.

3   "Save us! Save us!"

4   Cried Mrs. Davis.

1,2   The fire department got the call,

3,4   And the firemen saved them, one and all!

Thirty Days Has September

1   Thirty Days has September,

2   April, June, and November.

3   All the rest have thirty-one,

1   Except February alone,

2   And that has twenty-eight days clear,

3   And twenty-nine in each leap year.

Fooba Wooba John

I   Saw a snail chase a whale,

All   Fooba Wooba, Fooba Wooba,

I   Saw a snail chase a whale,

All   Fooba Wooba John.

I   Saw a snail chase a whale,

I   All around the water pail.

All   Hey, John, ho, John,

All   Fooba Wooba John.

2   Saw a frog chase a dog,

All   Fooba Wooba, Fooba Wooba,

2   Saw a frog chase a dog,

All   Fooba Wooba John.

2   Saw a frog chase a dog,

2   Sitting on a hollow log.

All   Hey, John, ho, John,

All   Fooba Wooba John.

3 Saw a flea kick a tree,

All Fooba Wooba, Fooba Wooba,

3 Saw a flea kick a tree,

All Fooba Wooba John.

3 Saw a flea kick a tree,

3 In the middle of the sea.

All Hey, John, ho, John,

All Fooba Wooba John.

4   Heard a cow say meow,

All   Fooba Wooba, Fooba Wooba,

4   Heard a cow say meow,

All   Fooba Wooba John.

4   Heard a cow say meow,

4   Then I heard it say bow-wow.

All   Hey, John, ho, John,

All   Fooba Wooba John.

The Lady with the Alligator Purse

1   Miss Lucy had a baby;

2   His name was Tiny Tim.

3   She put him in the bathtub

All   To see if he could swim.

1   He drank up all the water,

2   He ate up all the soap,

3   He tried to eat the bathtub,

All   But it wouldn't go down his throat.

1   Miss Lucy called the doctor,

2   The doctor called the nurse,

3   The nurse called the lady

All   With the alligator purse.

1   In walked the doctor,

2   In walked the nurse,

3   In walked the lady

All   With the alligator purse.

1   "Mumps," said the doctor.

2   "Measles," said the nurse.

3   "Nothing," said the lady

All   With the alligator purse.

1, 2   Out went the doctor,

2, 3   Out went the nurse,

All   Out went the lady

All   with the alligator purse.

A Note to the Teacher

Primary Concepts Readers' Theater scripts are a powerful way to help children develop fluent reading skills as they become acquainted with children's literature classics. Readers' Theater provides the following benefits:

- develops skill in pacing, articulation, phrasing, and expression in oral reading
- encourages children to monitor their own reading for fluency
- builds cooperative skills in a small group
- acquaints young readers with time-honored favorites from children's literature

Readers' Theater is the performance of literature that is read aloud expressively rather than acted. Because the goal is to perform the selections in front of a group, Readers' Theater gives children an incentive for reading familiar text over and over, thus improving their fluency.

Using the Scripts

Students work in small groups of two to four children. They either choose or are assigned one or more pieces to practice, and the part (1, 2, 3, or 4) each child should take. The number of parts is indicated by a symbol at the top of each script.

Practice Makes Perfect

Each child should be given his or her own script book. The group reads and rereads the text, perfecting their fluency, pacing, phrasing, and expression and the flow from one reader to the next. The group can listen to an audiotape model of the piece, or you may wish to model the reading yourself. For most children, the goal is to read the piece, not memorize it, but English language learners benefit from memorizing the text and then reading along.

Students typically listen critically to their own readings and try to improve with each reading. Members of the group should be encouraged to listen attentively and give each other feedback on the readings. Remind students how to give positive feedback by first telling what is working, then what might be improved and how. Students can write directly in the book, underlining words for special emphasis, or using slash marks to indicate pauses.

As the groups become proficient in their readings, you might want to encourage them to experiment with special ways to read the text:

- saying some words or phrases loudly and others softly
- slowing down or speeding up text
- shortening or lengthening pauses

Performance Time

After the children have practiced to near perfection, have them read selections in front of an audience: their classmates, another classroom, or parents. Consider inviting parents for a Readers' Theater Tea. Students will enjoy making the invitations. The formal tea will make all their hard work pay off with the applause of pleased parents.

While no costumes or props are required for these performances, children may wish to dress up in some special way. Hand movements can enhance the performance, as can simple musical accompaniments. However, bear in mind that the focus should be a celebration of reading.

Copyright

Every effort has been made to verify that all the selections in this book are in the public domain. Most appear in a variety of forms in a number of sources. Feel free to adapt the selections in any way you wish.

Other Resources

Readers' Theater script books and audiotapes are available in several genres. For these and other resources for teachers, please consult a Primary Concepts catalog or visit our website at **www.primaryconcepts.com.**